TEACH ME TO PRAY

A Beginner's Emotional Prayer Guide

Rebecca Puckett

ISBN 979-8-88943-963-9 (paperback)
ISBN 979-8-88943-964-6 (digital)

Christian Faith Publishing
832 Park Avenue
Meadville, PA 16335
www.christianfaithpublishing.com

Printed in the United States of America

Glory to our Father in Heaven who called
on my heart to share his love.
Dedicated to my children: Bennett, Avalyn, and Kenzie.

To the Parent/Guardian

The disciples asked Jesus to teach them how to pray as it was new to them. Children are also new to prayer, and what better time to start than now? As a parent, it is our job to teach our children how to pray. Repetition is typically taught to get them started, but why not give them a relationship they can grow in? Children look up to their parents or guardians to teach them. This book can help set an example you may not have been taught yourself.

My goal for this book is to help guide parents and children to work together to learn prayer as a relationship, not fancy words. Read the book to your child and help them to fill in the blanks in the free space on each page. Over time, they will start to pray on their own as they grow confident in talking to God.

Read to your Child

Praying is talking to God, your Father in Heaven. Just like here on earth, we talk things through. He wants to hear what you are feeling. You can tell him your joy, your anger too; he's here to listen, and you can tell him you're sorry too. He knows you make mistakes, and he's ready to forgive, just open up and tell him; you'll feel better in a jiff.

Index

Dear Lord, today I feel happy because______. I have what I need, I feel loved, and _____. Thank you for all of my blessings. I am grateful for the air in my lungs and the joy in my heart. Amen.

1 

I will be glad and rejoice in you; I will
sing the praises of your name, O Most
High. (Psalm 9:2 NIV)

2

Dear Lord, today I feel angry because____. Things are not going my way, and I feel ____. I don't want to be so angry, but I don't know what to do. Lord, help me to be calm and find peace in you. Amen.

3

Refrain from anger and turn from
wrath; do not fret—it leads only to evil.
(Psalm 37:8 NIV)

4

Dear Lord, today I feel scared because____. Lord, I know you are always there, but help me to be strong and trust that you will keep me safe. Amen.

So do not fear, for I am with you;
do not be dismayed, for I am your God.
I will strengthen you and help you; I
will uphold you with my righteous right
hand. (Isaiah 41:10 NIV)

Dear Lord, today I feel sad because____. I cry and I feel ____. I know you love me, but I need help to get through____. Amen.

7

The Lord is close to the brokenhearted and saves those who are crushed in spirit. (Psalms 34:18 NIV)

Worry

Dear Lord, today I feel worried because ____. I am anxious about ____. I know you have good plans for me Lord, please help me to take a breath and put my worries away. Amen.

9 

Do not be anxious about anything, but in every situation, by prayer and petition, with thanksgiving, present your requests to God. (Philippians 4:6 NIV)

10

Dear Lord, today I feel at peace. I feel joy and _____ in my heart. Your works are good, Lord. Even through my trials, I find peace in your presence. Thank you for your love and _____. Amen.

11 

I have told you these things, so that in me you may have peace. In this world you will have trouble. But take heart! I have overcome the world. (John 16:33 NIV)

Jealous

Dear Lord, today I feel jealous because_____. I see my friend has_____ and it makes me want to have it too. I know I should not want what my friend has. Lord, help me to guide my mind to finding joy in what I already have. I am grateful for_____. Amen.

13

Then he said to them, "Watch out! Be
on your guard against all kinds of greed;
life does not consist in an abundance
of possessions." (Luke 12:15 NIV)

Sorry

Dear Lord, I feel sorry for ____. Please forgive me for ____. I want to do better and learn from my mistakes. Lord, I will work on ____ and loving others as you do. Amen

15 

If we confess our sins, he is faithful and just and will forgive us our sins and purify us from all unrighteousness. (1 John 1:9 NIV)

Dear Lord, I am nervous about ____. I want to be strong and ____. I ask that you help me to trust in you and I give these nerves to you. Amen

17

Cast all your anxiety on him because
he cares for you. (1 Peter 5:7 NIV)

18

Dear Lord, I am excited for ___. Thank you for giving me ___. I am happy to have a Lord that loves me and blesses me. Amen

19

Take delight in the Lord, and he
will give you the desires of your heart.
(Psalm 37:4 NIV)

No matter what this day may bring, God, you love me through everything. Sometimes I'm high, sometimes I'm low, but your grace is overflowing. I know you won't let go. When life gets hard, that's when I learn. No matter what this day may bring, God, I thank you for everything. Amen.